The Running Promise

Author's copy
of my book some
corrections in process
I hope you enjoy it.
Elba War

The Running Promise

A memoir

By Elba Watkins

Acknowledgement

A special thanks to Erika Shukert, Michella Thomas, Jeremy Cowperthwaite and Janet Cowperthwaite, for taking time from their busy lives to read the book, and provide me with fantastic comments and invaluable feedback during the editing process.

Dedicated to all the women who once had a dream that seemed impossible, to those who have worked hard to make their dreams a reality, and to those who are still in the process of discovery. I hope my story will be inspirational. We each have a destiny to fulfill and the power to realize our destiny is within us throughout our lives. It is up to each of us to discover our power and to *believe* in it.

To my mom, in whose memory I started to run, and whose memory I hold close to my heart.

To my beautiful nieces who have always motivated me to do better.

To Jeremy Cowperthwaite, Noel Zaragoza, Priya Bendale, Hector Andrade, Catherine Tradd, Michella Thomas, Christina Macatee, and other mentors I have had throughout my life who have believed in me and encouraged me to grow and go beyond my comfort zones to discover a better me.

To my siblings who are and always have been my strongest supporters.

To all my *Team In Training* financial supporters who have made a difference in other peoples' lives and in my life.

Introduction

It was as if running was in my DNA, as if I knew it was going to happen. I dreamed about it and wrote about it, but somehow although it was in my mind I did not start running until I was 37 years old. There were a series of events that brought me to the beginning of this journey and I want to share with you some of these events, and some of my history with the hope that I might inspire you to find your passion. I hope you will consider running, but whatever your passion is, I hope it will bring the energy and happiness to your life as running has brought to mine for nearly ten years.

With the passing of time I have learned more and more how different and unique we humans are and how precious these gifts are. As you read this book, I encourage you to transform your view of the world for just a moment to perceive what you are about to read from the lens of my background. You may know others who have achievements that have been greater than mine, but to understand the real meaning of my words and my story, you have to see it from my point of view. It is all about each individual's journey in life. We all face different challenges, but most important is what we do with what life has put in front of us.

When I was younger, I used to day dream about running. Not even competitive running, but simply wanting to go the distance. But every time I wanted to start running there seemed to be a voice in my head that said I couldn't, so I didn't.

It was 2009 when life had become the hardest in many ways for me, and it was then the "I can't" voice in my mind turned into the "I must try" voice.

I was diagnosed with a tumor that needed to be removed. I spent a few weeks trying to figure things out, getting second opinions, and finally checking into the hospital. The tumor was located in my stomach and given that my mother died from stomach cancer, I was very worried and scared. My tumor was removed but as I reflected on the difficult times I was experiencing, not only with my health, but with so many other things, I felt more alone than ever and deeply sad and unsafe. Having lost both of my parents in a very short time, and having to adapt culturally to a society that I didn't feel I belonged to I was scared!

I felt I needed a reason to be alive. I wanted to help other people so that I could feel my own life was worth living. I found this purpose in running. I ran my first race in 2010 - the San Diego Rock 'n Roll full marathon with *Team In Training* for the Leukemia and Lymphoma Society. Every year since then, I have run the same race, but the half marathon. My goal in running each year has been to raise funds to support patients and their families who are going through the painful process of diagnosing and treating cancer, as well as to support research to find the cure that could have extended the life of my mother, and countless others.

My original motivation to start was to help others and make a difference in their lives, but I came to discover shortly into the journey that I had, in fact, helped myself... I had made a difference in my own life.

You may be experiencing something in your life that brings sadness, or has made you lose your way. I hope this story helps you realize how important your life is, and that you can find meaning and happiness by helping others and by exploring your own passion.

Table of Contents

Follow Your Destiny

"I have always believed that there is a reason for our existence, and every choice we make and every action we take will help us to get to know what that reason is."

Elba Watkins

Elba Watkins

My Background in Sports and in Life

was born in a small country town called Ejido, Oaxaca in Mexicali, Mexico. I was the youngest in a family of ten children, and even though we had very different personalities and some different ways of looking at life, thanks to my wonderful parents we shared very similar values.

Ever since I was a little girl, I remember looking up at everybody and listening to what they had to say, always respecting their opinions and thoughts but not saying much myself.

Years ago, the cultural belief was that girls were supposed to get married and have children, and boys were the powerful ones, expected to provide for their families, to work and learn, and not be allowed to cry. I remember seeing my brothers wearing basketball uniforms even though I don't remember going to see their games, but I wish I could have. I always wanted to do things differently, however I was not yet courageous enough to say anything.

As I was growing I had a periodic pain in my legs that would come and go. We didn't know its source therefore we could not control it. This came to be an obstacle for me. Whenever I would be ready to suggest something, my mom would say "If your legs hurt, maybe you shouldn't do it."

The Running Promise

Sports were not something that was seen as a family activity, or even part of the culture, especially for girls.

When I was about 4 years old my oldest brother bought me a tricycle. I rode it all the time and I loved it. Eventually my father gave me a bicycle. I remember riding my bicycle after school going back and forth just on our street, but it was fun. It had never occurred to me that riding a bicycle was a "sport", it was just a way to occupy my mind and stay active after school.

When I was in junior high, I would sometimes run as part of the school requirements, but no more than a mile and only once a week, so it could barely be considered running. I used to walk to school and back also, but that was my only exercise at that point in my life.

In high school I joined the school band to play the clarinet, and thus, sports were out of the picture again. I wanted to be part of the soccer team, but because my commute to school was so long, and I was so dependent on the school bus to take me home, soccer was not possible.

My parents paid an annual fee for the school bus to pick me up and take me to school. If I missed the bus, I would have to pay for public transportation, which I could not afford. I remember getting up at 4am to get ready and to walk to the bus stop. It took about 40 minutes to get to school. I would arrive very early and had to wait until classes started. It was a similar situation after school, so there was no way I could participate in soccer.

It wasn't until I started university that I began to think that running would be a fun thing to do, but I didn't yet feel comfortable. I was not used to going running and there was no place close to home to run. There was a desire to do it, but I didn't think I could, and once again I listened to my negative voice and didn't do it.

I now regret not pursuing it further when I was younger and my legs were stronger. When I graduated with my Engineering degree, I still had a strong feeling I should run. But again it seemed like a faraway kind of dream, an unreachable dream. I used to keep a diary back then and there were times when I would write as a day dream, as if it were true, "today I ran five kilometers, and I feel very happy. The truth is I didn't and there is an empty space inside because I couldn't do it." Reading that passage in my diary now makes me feel that running was something I was always meant to do. Why I believed that I couldn't, I do not know.

I now know that I could have, but then it seemed impossible. But the barrier was all in my mind. Perhaps it was the fact that I didn't see it being done, or perhaps it was the fact that I wasn't exposed to women in sports, but overall perhaps it was the fact that my thinking was negative about the possibility. I didn't believe I could do it.

"A positive thought can be the spark that inspires the realization that the dream that you once thought was impossible is possible."

Elba Watkins

It is interesting to me how our minds can either empower or abolish our power to act, allowing us to achieve great things that will bring happiness to our lives or leave us with poignant disappointment and sadness in our hearts. I see people around my age within the same environment with similar negative thoughts regarding their possibilities and I want to tell them: "Believe you can do it, or try it. Try not to be afraid to act, or take action despite the fear. We are all afraid at some moment in life, and it is what the fear makes us do that makes the difference. If you try, this courageous decision will change your life in a way you never thought possible."

Hope, Hope, We Cannot Lose Hope

My relationship with my mom was always special when I was growing up. As the youngest of ten, I ended up spending more time with her. We cooked together, and she would tell me stories from the past. We enjoyed spending time together. She taught me things like sewing, making art flowers, and making decorations for the home. She was the most creative person I have ever known - she could make art out of nothing.

My mother was also the most generous person in my world, she taught me the importance of sharing and disconnecting from material things. She would always put others first. If she had a small piece of food or something, she would share it equally among everybody, sometimes excluding herself. She was a beautiful soul and a beautiful woman.

In August of 1997 my mother was diagnosed with cancer. We didn't know much about cancer then. The doctor just told us that there was not much time left for her to live.

That August she started chemotherapy and all of my brothers and sisters were notified. We knew it was cancer, but we didn't want to lose faith. One of my sisters recommended that we take her to a natural medicine doctor, and we all agreed we would not tell my mom about her diagnosis right away.

We wanted her to believe that she was going to be OK. We had hope, and we wanted her to have hope. The chemotherapy treatments were regular, but in addition the natural doctor had recommended a special mud treatment, which consisted of mixing soil and water and spreading it on the affected area.

My mom and I when I was a child.

My dad prepared the mud and I assisted. It was hard for her and it was hard for us as this occurred every day. At the same time, we also tried a diet change to help her to feel better at the suggestion of the natural medicine doctor. We removed all red meats and added more vegetables. She started to lose weight rapidly and she also lost her hair due to the medications. She was diabetic, and we had to monitor her food and blood sugar very carefully as she almost went into a diabetic coma on several occasions.

My mom had always been very careful about not allowing us kids to see her without clothes. I had never seen my mom undressed when I was a child. When she felt sick because of the cancer, I would have to help her shower because she was so weak. It was something she saw as very special to her because there were no barriers. I hugged her and wished I could protect her. She would tell me, "You are my little angel." So often during this time I thought about her suffering. Her face had so much sorrow. I would wonder what she was thinking, what was in her mind. I still wonder if I could have done something else to make her days better, but I know she was holding on to her faith as much as I was. During all her times of agony, I never saw her cry out loud or complain, and I only saw tears coming from her eyes a few times.

Close to the end we decided to stop the mud treatment and the diet changes because we wanted her to have peace and to eat what she wanted. Seeing my mom like this was one of the most difficult experiences of my life.

My mom's battle with cancer ended at noon on May 23, 1998. She was my light and my reason to live, and I knew then that my whole world had changed. During the funeral I could not cry or speak. I saw her for the last time during the full night of the "velacion," which in my culture is the last time you will see your loved one. It is a full night where the body of the person who has passed away is there for friends and family to say their goodbyes one last time. After that night, there is a church service and then the body is taken to the cemetery.

After everyone left that night, I was in my room and it finally sunk in that I had lost my mom, that she was not there anymore, and she was gone forever. I cried and cried, and could not stop crying. My brother Lorenzo came and hugged me. My other siblings tried to help me as well, but at that point I just needed to cry.

Everyone was devastated, especially my dad. When my brother Juan was little my mom and dad made a promise to visit a cathedral in Mexico call San Juan de los Lagos. They made this promise because Juan was sick. They prayed for him to get better and in return for his health, they promised to visit the cathedral. But life got busy and they were never able to fulfil that promise. Some of my siblings suggested my dad should go and they accompanied him. He needed to get away and making this special journey would help bring him peace. I couldn't go on that trip because of work commitments and I found myself more alone, physically and emotionally, than I had ever been before.

I felt lost in life after my mother was gone. The time following her death was one of the hardest I've experienced so far.

Elba Watkins

My Parents' Special Wedding

My parents never had a wedding ceremony with a big white dress in a church and all those nice things that traditional weddings have. My mom wanted one and she said it many times. In the year 2000 my parents were going to celebrate 50 years of marriage and they wanted to have the wedding then. My mom had asked us to start planning it, and my siblings and I would have liked to have the celebration, but she was diagnosed in 1997 and passed away the next year, so the wedding could not take place.

However, I did experience the wedding on February 17, 2002. It was so vivid, so peaceful. My dad was there in that beautiful church, there were roses everywhere, white ribbons hung from one bench to the other. All of my siblings and I dressed for the occasion. My nieces and nephews were there too. My mom appeared at the door of the church, coming to meet my dad. She was wearing the unique dress that she dreamed about, just as she wanted, white and beautiful.

There they were, together in front of God, and it was the most beautiful wedding. There was an atmosphere of serenity, ineffable peace, love, and unity.

That Sunday morning when I woke up from my dream, I received the phone call that my father had passed away.

I had made prior arrangements to visit him on Monday, so when he died that Sunday morning I was devastated once again. My life after that day was dedicated to observing other people's lives, almost as if mine didn't exist. I felt like I was not living. I was afraid - very afraid - for many years.

Happiness

"Happiness is something that needs to be discovered."

Elba Watkins

F or years after my mother's death I was unable to find my own happiness. This was the point in my life when if someone asked me what brought me joy, I could not give a concrete answer. I would say things like "I am happy when I can help others," or "I am happy when I am close to my family," or other similar generic things.

I thought I needed to know what made me happy, with certainty and confidence, and without hesitation. One day I was looking for affirmations in a podcast and I found the perfect one. It said "knowing what you want sometimes takes careful deliberation, I have the right to say no, knowing what you want is good, and healthy." I downloaded it and started listening.

After deep deliberation about how to seek happiness - what specific activities to choose and what specific actions to take - I realized everyone must seek, on the deepest level, what it is that will fulfill their heart to create joy. And that is when I discovered running. But why did running make me happy? Perhaps it is because when I run I get a fair chance to win, or because my toughest competitor is me, or maybe it is simply because I can do it. I know my legs are there and I can feel them when I run. Perhaps it is the fact there is a new me every time I try harder.

Running is also one of the ways for me to be in touch with nature; to get energy from outside and turn it in to energy inside myself. I like running because, despite the pain, it is something I can personally use to help others. It is through deep deliberation I have come to this wonderful state of mind when I run. People are so diverse and there are so many different ways to make them happy. We have to find those ways, hold them close to our hearts, dream with them, and live by them. The possibilities are endless. After discovering what makes us happy we can then make decisions and take action.

Supporting Leukemia and Lymphoma Society (LLS) by running the San Diego Rock 'n' Roll 2010 full marathon for the first time was a major decision for me.

Sometimes we are part of a bigger plan when a universal energy moves us in inexplicable ways, and sometimes we just have to trust that the ideas and dreams that appear in our minds will eventually lead us to the best future..."God is good."

In December 2009, I learned I had a tumor in my stomach that was causing pain and bleeding. I was told by the doctor I needed surgery, and I was in a hospital bed sooner than I expected. At first I didn't know if the growth was cancerous or benign. Given that my mom died of cancer I was very worried, and I already had mixed emotions about life and things around me.

Thankfully, my tumor was benign and that was good news, but it still needed to be removed. Being in that hospital bed

13

made me reflect about my life and my dreams, both past and the present. Coincidentally, before the surgery, I had been thinking about my mom a lot, and I felt I needed to do something to change my life. I started to remember how much I wanted to run in the past and how that thought had always been present, but I had never done anything about it. I had ignored the thought for many years.

And then one day, without looking for it and as if someone had planned it for me, I saw a Leukemia and Lymphoma Society (LLS) Team In Training advertisement inviting people to join their running team. I decided to go to their opening meeting to learn more. Upon learning the amount of money I needed to raise I had some concerns but decided to give it my best try.

In January, almost four weeks after my surgery, I was already signed up and on my way to my first training session.

The Leukemia and Lymphoma Society (LLS) is an association that provides blood cancer information, and provides support for patients, survivors and families. LLS helps cancer patients with treatments, but the goal is to end cancer. And while they are working to reach that goal, LLS helps many people to have a better quality of life – both patients and families – during treatment. LLS also dedicates a lot of resources to finding the cure in medical trials and new research.

During my early days with Team In Training I remember thinking, "what am I doing here?" I have never run long distance before, much less a marathon. Maybe I do not belong here. But I was willing to give all I had to prove I could do something big to help and create hope for others. Perhaps all the years of wanting to run were for a reason, and perhaps I was meant to do this. Perhaps I was pursuing my happiness.

Training Begins

The team received training schedules for the full and half marathons. We knew what to do during the week to train on our own. The training would include running days, alternative exercise days using gym equipment such as the elliptical machine, and rest days. The days were also divided by running hills and doing intervals (going fast and slow for short periods of time consecutively to increase speed). The weekend schedule was to go on a long run as a team at a pre-determined location, and to always rest on Sunday.

For every long team training session, I would wake up early on Saturday morning to meet the team. Every weekend run was the longest I had ever done until that point. First, we started with three miles, then four, five, six, seven, ten, etc., all the way up to 18 miles and they were all hard. During the training sessions I remember meeting a woman. She had shared with me the passing of her beloved husband, and she was emotionally drained, always sad and living a day at a time. For some reason I connected with her and we ran together many times even though she was faster than me. After getting to know her I started to believe she was an angel on my journey.

To experience what a race day would be like, LLS had signed the team up for an 8K race that started in Balboa Park.

16

This was my first race ever. I remember it was raining that day, but I enjoyed every moment of the race.

During the session when I was training for 14 miles, I knew that I had just passed the half marathon distance. Running 14 miles was big considering I had never done a half marathon before.

All the people in Team In Training were very supportive of me. Every running session, we had an inspirational moment where we could hear stories of each other's lives relating to the experiences with cancer and the reasons we were running.

Most of the people running were connected one way or another to cancer. Some people were survivors, and some had family members that were struggling as we were training, and some others knew a loved one who had lost the battle. No matter what the story or the reason for being there was, we were there to support each other. This was very important for me and I felt for the first time in a long time in my life. I was doing something special. I was there to help save lives.

Elba Watkins

Mother's Day Run

I distinctly remember a 16 mile training run on Mother's Day, and the person I was running with, Melissa, ran faster than me. I didn't have a map and got lost on the course and ended up running more than a mile longer than the 16 miles I was supposed to log that weekend. My mind was invaded by memories of my mom, my legs were exhausted, and I started to believe I was not going to be able to do it. I started crying big tears when I finally spotted the people from the team.

I got there, running at a very slow pace, almost walking, but I finished. I stopped when I got to the grass and collapsed there and cried even harder, not able to stop. Naturally, everybody wanted to support and help me, but I had no words. I couldn't express all the emotions I was experiencing. I told them how afraid I was of not being able to finish. It was too intricate to explain.

The following week I ran my longest run of that season 18 miles. My mind was fresh and I was feeling better. I didn't get lost and I ended the run feeling more confident I could complete the 26.2 mile marathon on June 6, 2010. This run was particularly satisfying not only because it was the longest, but also because of the special route. All Team In Training members from different locations were gathered for this race. We took the train from Solana Beach to Oceanside on a Saturday morning from 6:33 to 6:54, a 21 minute ride, and then ran back 18 miles with the most beautiful scenic view.

From all the stories I heard during my years of running, I remember a few that have stayed close to my heart. One of them was about a seven year old girl who spoke to us on a morning before a training run. She spoke about the experiences she had been through having had more than seven brain surgeries. She talked about the days at the hospital, the kindness of the nurses, and her family's routines. As we listened to her she sounded like an adult with a much higher level of maturity and understanding than she should have in her short life dealing with cancer.

From my first Team In Training meeting I had a strong and determined realization I was there to give something to others. I was there to help save lives and to prevent other families from losing their loved ones. I was there to help people find a way to have access to medicine that would help treat cancer, and I was there to help find the cure. I was there to give, but along the way, I received so much more.

I learned many things about running, such as how to use the foam roller, how to properly hydrate, and how to cross train to prevent injuries. I met wonderful people who dedicate their precious time in life to this cause. I heard so many warm stories that I keep close to me. I knew the training was going to be difficult. I got injured and had to slow down for four weeks. It was painful, but I felt what I gave up for the experience was nothing. What I received were lifetime memories.

Elba Watkins

Before the 2010 Rock 'n' Roll Marathon there were two days of a Health and Sports Exposition (Expo) at the San Diego Convention Center, where you could find anything you can imagine regarding running. This is where I picked up my running number (bib).

There were lots of vendors showing the latest items in running gear, shoes, equipment etc., as well as the latest on nutritional food for runners. During this event you also get to know the race course, the medals that will be awarded, information about the race day such as road closures, where to park, and other things. You could also choose to change your race type. For example, if you signed up for the full marathon but decided to run the half instead, they changed it for you there.

Throughout these two days there were also professional runners who signed autographs and spoke on panels. The 2010 Expo was my first time experiencing an event like this. LLS had a booth with all the information about the organization, where runners could get signs for family members and their supporters to write messages to use at the race for encouragement. They also had signs that you could wear which said, "I run in memory of" or "I run in honor of." I chose the sign "I run in Memory of" and filled it in with my mom's name, Magdalena.

As part of the LLS running season closure there was an Inspiration Dinner. Participating runners from all over the country were together in one place at this dinner. They shared the fundraising goals, told very inspirational stories, and there were enough carbohydrates to load the runners with good fuel for the race day! This dinner was very special for me as I was getting ready to do something I had never done before. As with everything new, there was some fear associated with the experience, but after listening to how meaningful this was, I felt I was mentally prepared for the challenge. There were a lot of tears involved in the dinner as you heard the sad stories of those who had lost loved ones, but there was also joy and positive energy as you heard the stories of those who survived. After hearing about the struggles people had been through, running seemed to be the easy part of the journey, despite the pain and aches that came with it.

Elba Watkins

First Marathon: 2010 San Diego Rock and Roll

FULL MARATHON

June 6th arrived and there I was at five in the morning waiting for the full marathon to start. I was nervous as we all get when we are about to do something we have never done before. I felt I could run the race given my training, but the longest I had run to date was 18 miles. Getting to 26.2 miles was going to be a large task and I was excited about the challenge.

As agreed, I met with the team at Balboa Park near the starting line of the race and patiently waited for the start time. We were talking to one another and we eventually started to stretch. Meanwhile I had an important goal in mind - "I will finish this marathon running. I will not walk. I will finish running." This was my goal.

The race began. I felt as if I started going as fast as I could, but it still seemed slow. I felt people were passing me. I soon realized I needed to slow down even more. I did not have a racing watch to set my pace, but I could feel it. After three miles or so I slowed down to a pace I could maintain, and it seemed I was more comfortable there. At ten miles I felt good. I passed the 13-mile mark - my first half marathon ever

22

- and I felt great! I kept running and passed the 15-mile and then the 18-mile mark. At this point I knew I was as far as I had trained, and that simple thought started to influence my mind, and fear started to invade my thinking.

I felt tired but I remembered my goal, "I will finish this marathon running, I will not walk, I will finish running." I was now at 20 miles and my pace was very slow, but I kept pushing. At mile 23 I was almost ready to give up when I found a friend in the race. Chris and I had worked together before and he and his wife had donated to my run, but I didn't know he was running the full marathon. It was a surprise. I said hello to him and he started to tell me he had qualified to run the Boston Marathon, he ran it earlier in April, and his company had sponsored him.

During our conversation I kept running with him but I noticed I was slowing him down a lot. I told him I was almost ready to walk to the end but my goal was to finish this race running. However, I was so tired that I didn't think I would be able to do it. He told me not to worry, that he wasn't running this one for time. He said he would run with me and we would both finish this race running. I thanked him for his encouragement and was able to keep running for the rest of the race. I am forever thankful that he stayed with me and inspired me.

I ran the San Diego Rock 'n' Roll 2010 full marathon in a little less than 5 hours and raised close to two thousand dollars to support LLS. I had a great feeling inside that came from helping others. I also had a tremendous feeling of accomplishment and remember saying "if I can finish a marathon I can do anything."

Elba Watkins

The Ten Year Running Promise

R unning my first marathon gave me the confidence to transform my life. When I finished the race, my body was in pain but my mind had feelings of happiness, exhaustion, and great accomplish-ment. It was not at that exact moment, but after reflecting on that day over and over for a few weeks I made a promise to myself that I was going to continue to run for ten years. I would run and offer my healthy legs to raise money for such a special cause. It was a promise to honor my mom's memory, a promise to the people I had met who battled cancer that year with whom I felt strongly connected, and a promise to myself.

In June 2011 and June 2012, I ran the San Diego Rock 'n' Roll Marathon again, but this time only the half marathon. These races finished close to Sea World and the half marathon course was closer to the ocean. The organizers eventually changed the course to Finish at Petco Park and later to Waterfront Park. In 2012 I also ran the Los Angeles Rock 'n' Roll half marathon.

Start Line at Los Angeles Rock 'n' Roll Marathon, 2012.

By 2012 I felt I had some experience and I repeated the same preparation for racing. I signed up for races and committed to getting up early on most of my Saturdays from January to June for those long training runs. It was typical for me to get up at 5:30 am. I would have coffee and a nutritional bar and would meet with the team.

All long training runs had a lot of volunteers and there were water stations throughout the route marked on the map. The Health and Sports Expo at the San Diego Convention Center happened every year. The night before the race we had the Inspiration Dinner that was very special, and very full of carbohydrates.

During my journey into this new world of running, I had learned about Meb Keflezighi. Meb is a professional San Diego runner and his story is very inspirational. In his book *Run to Overcome,* Meb describes what victory means to him and how he overcame difficult times.

Meb won a silver medal in the Athens, Greece 2004 Olympics and had won the New York Marathon in 2009. I knew he was preparing for the London Olympics in 2012 and he was going to be at the San Diego Rock'n'Roll Marathon.

During the 2012 San Diego Rock 'n' Roll Marathon, I remember seeing Meb Keflezighi for the first time in the convention center at the Health and Sports Expo. Every year my bib theme was "God is Good" and it was written on my bib. I heard Meb was signing bibs and I asked him to sign mine. When he saw my bib he asked, "Did you write that?" I said yes and then he wrote "God is GREAT!!! Run to win!" He won the half marathon that year with an amazing time of 1:03:11. I felt honored to have run the same course as him.

Another runner I have learned from and have come to admire is Wilma Rudolph. Her inspirational story is one of the most beautiful and powerful stories I have ever heard.

Wilma was born in 1940, in the state of Tennessee. She was born into poverty in the racially segregated south. She suffered from early childhood illnesses, including pneumonia, and she develop muscle weakness resulting in an inability to move her left leg due to poliomyelitis when she was only four years old. Even though she recovered from polio, she lost strength in her left leg and foot and had to wear a brace until she was eight years old. She also wore an orthopedic shoe to support her foot for a couple of years.

Wilma started her own journey in sports playing basketball, but it was not long before she discovered that her passion was running. At the 1960 Summer Olympics in Rome, Italy, Wilma competed in three events: the 100-meter and 200-meter sprints, as well as the 4 × 100-meter relay. She won gold medals in each of these events and became the first American woman to win three gold medals in a single Olympic Games.

In the opening heat of the 200 meter dash Wilma set a new Olympic record of 23.2 seconds, after following that with a clocking of 24 seconds in the final she was consider the fastest woman in history at that time.

After learning about Meb and Wilma's stories I felt very inspired and loved running even more.

My Road to Boston

The Boston Marathon is always held on Patriots' Day, the third Monday of April. This race started in 1897, is the oldest annual marathon in the world, and is considered one of the most famous. Many athletes from around the globe aspire to be part of this marathon. The race runs through eight Massachusetts cities and towns: Hopkinton, Ashland, Framingham, Natick, Wellesley, Newton, Brookline, and Boston.

The Boston Marathon is also known for being difficult because of the hills throughout the course. Near Newton, a particular difficult hill around the 20 mile mark, has the popular nickname "heartbreak hill."

The Boston Marathon is unique because not just anyone can just sign up for it and hope to finish it. You must participate in a qualifying race and you have to meet the minimum qualifying time for your age and gender, or support a charity organization.

I had known Jeremy for some time and he was a great friend. He was a long-time runner and he supported my running efforts. Another one of the angels on my journey, he was always kind, and always a supportive and caring person. He has been by my side to encourage me, to help me believe in myself, and to help me grow.

It was 2012 when Jeremy told me he thought I could qualify to run the Boston Marathon if I trained for it. Since entrance to the Boston Marathon was based on speed and time I told him I didn't think I could qualify. He said, "You can do it if you want it hard enough and if you train for it."

And with that the seed was planted. I wanted to do it. I started to look into the qualification time for my age group and the requirements needed for the marathon. I found out it was too late to try to qualify for Boston 2013, but I would prepare and train for Boston 2014.

I made the decision that fall to try to qualify and selected the Arizona Rock 'n' Roll Marathon as my qualifying race. Based on the Boston Standard for a woman my age, I needed to run the marathon in three hours and 45 minutes to qualify. Would I be able to do it? I didn't know if I was capable of running a full marathon that fast. The only full marathon I had completed to that moment was the San Diego Rock 'n' Roll, which I knew took me almost five hours. The required qualifying time of three hours and 45 minutes seemed monumental but I believed I could do it. At the very least I was willing to try!

In his book *Talent is Overrated,* Geoff Colvin speaks about deliberate practice. "Deliberate practice is characterized by several elements, each worth examining. It is activity designed specifically to improve performance, often with a teacher's help; it pushes the practicer just beyond, but not way beyond, his or her current limits; it can be repeated a lot; feedback on results is continuously available; it's highly demanding mentally, whether the activity is purely intellectual, such as chess or business-related activities, or heavily physical, such as sports; and it isn't much fun." I read this book and learned that coaching, a lot of practice, and constant feedback to adjust your practice can help improve performance, not only in sports, but in other areas too. This is exactly what I experienced when I was training to qualify for the Boston race. What I did at that time is what Colvin calls "Deliberate Practice." First I decided to reach the goal of qualifying for the Boston Marathon. Jeremy became my coach. One thing he would say when I felt tired or didn't see immediate results was, "you can only get better at running by running." It is that simple: a lot of repetition and adjustment along the way with the feedback I received eventually made a great difference and allowed me to reach my goal to qualify for the Boston Marathon. Some of the feedback I received, for example, was that I needed to do longer runs, to do more hills, to select the right hill areas to run, to find out the right numbers of repetitions for the interval training days, etc.

September was my first month of training and I started slowly. I asked Jeremy if he would help me create a training plan and he kindly agreed. After that, I was off and (literally) running on my own every week, up to five miles each day.

The plan was to do longer runs than just the regular five miles a day, but while I tried to stick to the plan, my back was not cooperating. It had started to hurt and eventually I went to physical therapy. After a few weeks I started to see improvement and I was very excited and wanted to push harder.

In the beginning of December 2012, Jeremy was diagnosed with melanoma on one of his ears, and we were both very scared.

The results of a biopsy had been positive and he had to go through removal of part of his ear and then another biopsy to ensure enough had been removed. We had to wait for the results. In the meantime, I was training and I ran every long run as hard as I could.

I wanted to do it for Jeremy. He had been an inspiration for me, was a great supporter, and a good friend. I knew it would mean a lot to him if I qualified, perhaps as much as it would mean to me. With every mile I ran I prayed he would be alright. I asked for another chance for him.

Just before Christmas Jeremy received the good news that he was OK! I was so happy to hear that news!

During Christmas dinner in 2012, in the house built by my father where I had lived as a child in Mexico, my family and I were writing our resolutions for the New Year on paper. We had cut the paper into the shape of a Christmas ornament. I had the idea to write down our dreams on the ornaments and to keep them with us through the year as a form of motivation to keep us going. We wrote them, and we shared them with one another. Mine was a simple phrase "26.2 @3.45 in 2013." It was a simple statement that contained a huge dream, qualifying for the 2014 Boston Marathon.

"26.2 miles at 3 hours and 45 minutes in 2013", a small sentence that capture a huge dream, was my resolution for the new year.

Last Long Training Run

"Do not let anything or anyone stop you, not even your own thoughts."

Elba Watkins

January 2013 arrived quickly and I needed to continue my training. It was two weeks before the marathon and I was preparing to do the last of my long runs of 19 miles. It was a cold Sunday morning. I had put my running gear on, and I had planned to run as fast as I could to try to simulate the race day.

The first ten miles went well, and around the 13-mile point Jeremy spotted me from his car. He brought water for me and wanted to say hi (something he kindly used to do through my training runs). He told me he was planning to go to the gym and we agreed to meet later for breakfast.

I kept on running and I was making good time, but at about 17 miles into the run - I don't know how it happened exactly - I fell down.

I was running fast and due to the speed, I couldn't put my hands down in time to stop my body. My face went directly into the cement and I felt my glasses pushing into my eyes and then breaking. I could feel blood running down my face.

A bicyclist who was passing by stopped, told me his name was Jason, and he asked if I wanted him to call 911. I said I was fine, that I was close to home, and that I was going to call a friend or run home.

He looked at me very puzzled and told me I really needed to go to a hospital. I repeated telling him I was OK. I thanked him and started to walk. Luckily, I had my phone with me and I called Jeremy a few times, but unfortunately, he was at the gym and didn't answer the first few calls.

I continued walking and kept trying to call him. I can remember I was not in any pain. I was in shock after what had happened to me and, in my mind, I started to think maybe I needed to go to the emergency room.

As I walked I remember approaching a supermarket entrance. I was going to cross the road and a car almost ran into me. At that moment I started to think I was not feeling all that well. Soon after, I saw Jeremy's car approaching me from the other side of the street. I kept walking and he made a U-turn to meet me. When I first saw him, he said he received my many messages and he was very worried. He asked me what happened, followed by a quick and worrisome "we need to take you to a hospital."

He took me to the emergency room at the nearest hospital. I remember waiting for a while before anyone could see me. I started to feel cold and my eye and nose started to hurt. I remember filling out a lot of forms before they finally called me in. The nurses immediately gave me pain medicine then cleaned up my face and took some x-rays. I was told my nose was broken and they needed to put some glue (rather than stitches) near my eye. They informed me I was lucky that parts of my glasses hadn't gone into my eye. Before leaving, I went to the restroom and I saw my face for the first time in the mirror. The areas surrounding my eye were red/purple-ish, as if somebody had hit me, and my nose was a bit deformed. I was a little bit emotional at that moment.

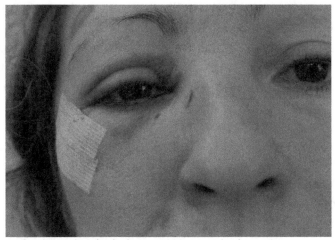

After the accident that broke my nose during my last long training run.

Jeremy and I left the hospital late, after 3PM and I had run more than 16 miles without having any breakfast or lunch. I was hungry, so we decided to go to a Vietnamese restaurant to get some warm pho. While we were waiting for the food at the restaurant, I stood up to go to the restroom and I almost fainted. It felt like everything was moving and that I was going to fall again. Jeremy held me, and it passed.

The next day, Monday, was supposed to be the start of my taper (reducing the length of training runs to prepare for the race) but, of course, I couldn't run for a few days so I did cross training at the gym for the rest of the week. I visited my doctor that Monday as well, and he sent me to a specialist to look at my broken nose.

I saw the doctor for me nose that same week and also visited my optometrist. Everything seemed to be healing well except it seemed that the skin around my nose was sinking more and more. The doctor recommended surgery, otherwise the bones would heal unevenly and cause respiratory problems in the future.

I told the doctor that I had the marathon to run in a week and we agreed to have the surgery the Monday after the race. We couldn't wait too long because the bones would heal incorrectly.

I was absolutely amazed to see my body heal as much as it did in two weeks. The red and purple of my eye was mostly gone, and I felt much better. I did some small runs that last week but not much.

For a few days the thought of not running the race crossed my mind, but I was feeling better and decided to continue as planned.

Qualifying Race Arizona

T he weekend of the Arizona qualifying race finally arrived. I was still anxious about my nose and my accident but I was also excited for the opportunity. I was a day away from perhaps the most important race of my running endeavor up to that point.

On Friday I picked up my bib and went to the Phoenix Convention Center for the Expo. I enjoyed my time there. It was a tradition that I was used to and I looked forward to it before each race. As the hours passed by, I became a little more nervous. I thought things were starting to hurt, somehow more so than before, but it was all in my mind.

I decided to dedicate this race to Jeremy, he is a two time cancer survivor and I thought how much he has been an inspiration for me to run and to try to qualify for the Boston Marathon. Thus I added a tag that said "In honor of: Jeremy" to my bib.

Jeremy suggested that I look to see if there were going to be pacers in the race. Pacers are typically very good runners who run at a set pace slower than they are capable of and volunteer to help others achieve their target speed goals. We looked at the Expo and found they did have pacers, so I signed up for a 3:40 group. This was faster than the time I needed, but I figured from the ones available, a 3:40 pacer was the best choice for me.

Pacer and group for 3:40 marathon, I started the race with them.

From then the plan was to stay with the pacer for as long as possible, and hopefully for the whole marathon. A time of 3:40 sounded ambitious, but as they say, "if you want to get to the moon, you may as well shoot for the stars and you may land on the moon."

Jeremy and I drove the marathon course to get familiar with it and we developed a plan for where to meet during and after the race.

The night before the race, as I was preparing all my things glasses, sun screen, attaching my bib to my shirt, etc. I kept telling myself "I will qualify in this race. Nothing is going to stop me, and I will qualify in this race. I will run 3:45 or better." I was very excited, and it was hard to fall asleep. It seemed that my body hurt somehow, but now when I think back, it was all about my state of mind.

The day of the race, January 20, 2013, was a fantastic day in Phoenix, Arizona. It was perfect weather to run 26.2 miles. I was cold at first, but I knew I would warm up quickly. I kept telling myself over and over "I will qualify in this race, I will qualify in this race." My mind wanted to hesitate, but I thought "Do not let anything stop you, you have prepared for this for a long time, you can do it."

I started to run right next to my pacer, just as Jeremy suggested. It felt very easy at first and I wanted to go faster than the pacer, but I did not. I saw Jeremy at the ten mile mark. I was smiling, and I remember saying, "This is easy." I was confident, still felt fresh, and had a big smile on my face. I kept that pace for a while.

Then at the 18 mile mark I saw Jeremy again and told him I thought I had a chance. Of course, by now I was feeling tired but was pushing as hard as I could, pushing hard enough that I was still with the pacer. He said "yeah, you can do this, I will see you at the 20th mile."

Part of our plan was for Jeremy to run the last six miles with me, and so we agreed to meet at mile 20.

When I arrived at the 20 mile point I was tired and almost out of energy. Jeremy joined me just in time as I had started to lose my pacer and I was slowing down. Jeremy kept encouraging me. I told him I was tired and wasn't sure if I could do it. He told me "come on - you can do this - you have worked very hard for it, and you are almost there, come on!" I kept running as fast as I could, and it was the harder than I had ever run before, but at that point the pace was slower than at the start. For more than five miles Jeremy was there with me, and his words of encouragement made the time go faster. He knew more than anyone how important this was to me.

Jeremy's words "you can do this, you have worked very hard for this, come on" are words I will never forget. With the finish line approaching, Jeremy left the course and I continued. I was tired, but I tried one more time to push myself a little harder - just a little more. I told myself, "just a little more Elba, you can do this, you have worked very hard for this" and as I crossed the finish line I saw the clock with my time and it said 3:42:05!

After I picked up my medal and got a drink I started looking for Jeremy, and there he was, waiting for me on the other side. He saw me and ran towards me and we hugged each other. He said "you did it! I knew you would!" I smiled and tears of joy were running down my cheeks. I said I couldn't believe it... did I just qualify for the Boston Marathon? I kept thanking Jeremy for his encouragement during the last six miles. I do not know if I could have done it without his words of encouragement.

This experience taught me a lesson about life, hard work, and achieving goals. Sometimes we are so close and all we need are words of encouragement to get there.

I am not sure if Jeremy knows just how much he did for me that day. Not only did he show me his support, but he also helped create a memory that will stay with me forever. He taught me that to help others achieve their goals we should extend a hand and offer words of encouragement. This may be all that is needed when there are difficult moments.

When I was on my way back to San Diego I met a lady at the airport who was 90 years old. We chatted during the flight and we exchanged emails. I told her my story and she told me hers. She was living alone and traveling to visit her daughter and sister. I believe you learn from every person you encounter in your life and the accumulation of experiences forms the person you are. She taught me that no matter what your age is and what happens to you, life is still beautiful if you are positive and enjoy the little things it brings you.

Immediately after my return I had the surgery for my nose. It was not a long procedure, but the bones were starting to heal and they had to move them so they would be in the right position. The doctor had to insert gauze to my nose and I had to leave it in there for a week. The first night was very difficult. It felt as if I could not breathe, and at the same time, I felt like I was starting to catch a cold. I was worried and I called the doctor, who assured me everything was all right. I was very fortunate to be able to get help and support from my doctor and my friends during this time.

After the surgery, I decided to rest for a while to recuperate and I got better very quickly.

I had signed up to run the San Diego Rock 'n' Roll half marathon for the fourth time, and I started training around the second week of February, 2013. I frequently ran at lunch or after work. People at work knew I had qualified for Boston and that I was running to raise funds for LLS, and they were very supportive. Many of my colleagues supported me every year and I am very grateful for that.

My journey with the San Diego Rock 'n' Roll half marathon and my Team In Training experience continued that year. There were times when I ran with my team and there were times when I trained on my own because of work travel or family commitments, but I was part of the team and my heart and my legs were dedicated to the cause.

In April I had to go to China for a business trip so I had to train at the hotel gym. It was not quite as fun, but I logged the miles. On April 15, 2013 at about 3:00PM Boston time, and early morning the next day in Shenzhen, China, due to the time zone difference, I received a strange call from a friend.

I did not reach the phone in time and checked the voice message. It was a close friend from work. She had called and left the following message "Are you OK? Are you running Boston this year? It seems you are not at work and I am worried about you."

I could not make sense of the message, but I remembered the Boston Marathon was happening at that time. I turned on the TV and heard the news about the bombings. I reached out to my friend and let her know I was traveling in China and that I had qualified for Boston the following year.

I was very moved by what had happened in Boston. I had just gone through a hard experience to qualify and I started to think about people and runners in Boston at that moment who had gone through so much to get there. I could not fathom how hard it must have been to have that experience to not be able to finish the race or to learn that your loved ones were injured or dead.

I followed the news closely and shared with my colleagues in China how significant the situation was for me. I knew it was late in the race when the bombings occurred, and a lot of the people still running at that time were people like me who were fundraising for a cause. The basic thought of what they may have gone through was painful to me. I prayed for their comfort and peace, for the healing of those injured, and for the families and friends of those who had lost their lives. My own Boston experience became even more personally meaningful on that fateful day.

San Diego Rock 'n' Roll 2013 Half Marathon

After qualifying for Boston, I still didn't know if I was going to be selected to run because I was told sometimes there are too many qualifiers and the field is selected on fastest qualifying times and the maximum number of runners allowed. My qualifying standard time, based on my age was 3:45, and I had qualified with 3:42, so I thought I may have a chance, but I was not sure. It all depended on the number of qualifying runners and their times.

I was not sure how the selection process worked, but I knew I was going to apply as soon as the window opened. In the meantime, I had already signed up and was training for the San Diego Rock 'n' Roll half marathon, and I had been fundraising for LLS since the beginning of the year.

One day in the beginning of May, my niece Gloria did something that touched my heart. Every year she would do a fundraising event to earn extra money for vacations or for personal needs, but this time she decided to give all the money she raised to my LLS cause. It was such a beautiful act. She put in so much time and effort and she gave all the proceeds away - everything. Her actions showed me and others her character, her generosity, and her love. She

44

helped create a memory that I will never forget and for which I am forever grateful.

She wrote the following words on my fundraising page:

"Because you are a person who fights for your cause, who works hard to better the world around you, who lives selflessly, who inspires positive change; because we, as your family (and as your fans), love you, support you, and want to see you achieve all of your goals; because there are good people in this world who are happy to donate their hard-earned money to support a good cause, and to help a friend; for all of these reasons, Tia, our family and our friends here in Santa Paula, would like to donate what we've been able to gather together for your fundraising page. We love you! Have a great, awesome marathon!" Gloria.

My heart sings when I think back. During this year I felt this act of generosity made my donations to LLS so much more meaningful. Gloria made all the difference in my contributions but most importantly she touched my soul and made me feel blessed and loved. In a way. She also showed me that giving everything without expectation of anything in return demonstrates unconditional love.

Boston Marathon 2014 Preparation

The registration for the 2014 Boston Marathon began in September 2013. I submitted my qualifying time and my application as soon as the window opened. As a mentioned before, I had heard that in some cases even if you met the qualifying standard you may not get in. It all depended on how fast your qualifying time was and how many people had signed up that year.

I also heard that because of what happened in the 2013 Boston Marathon, a lot of people were going to be running in 2014. So I submitted my application, but I was not sure if I was going to get into the race.

Despite not knowing whether I was going to be selected, I decided to begin training and started doing a simple five mile run each day.

It was the beginning of October when I received my confirmation letter in the mail - I was going to be part of the 2014 Boston Marathon!

I was so happy to receive the confirmation letter! I knew there were going to be a lot of people going to Boston so I decided to book my trip right away to make sure we had the best possible rates on airfare and hotels, as it can get very expensive later on.

Again, Jeremy volunteered to create a training plan for me, and this time it was more challenging than before. The plan consisted of running an easy route, then hills, then an easy route and then one focusing on speed. Saturday was cross training or an easy run, Sunday was always my long run, and Monday was my only day off. He also recommended I start a weight training plan.

When the Sunday runs became longer, Jeremy was always there. He brought water and checked on me to make sure I was ok. He was very supportive.

Elba Watkins

Good Luck from a Special Friend

I had been training hard for the race for a long time, and now it was the final week. I started to taper off and couldn't believe the day had almost arrived.

On Thursday, a day before leaving for Boston, I received a box in the mail. I didn't know what it was and when I opened it, there was a "Womble" girl. A friend of mine had sent it as a good luck charm. "The Wombles" was an English TV show from many years ago, and this Womble girl was made for my friend when she was a child by her grandmother. It held a lot of meaning for her and she sent it from San Francisco to San Diego just to give me good luck in the marathon. This was such a nice act and I felt very special.

Lucky Charm Womble Girl.

On Friday Jeremy and I took a flight from San Diego to Chicago, and then from Chicago to Boston. We took the Womble girl with us. During the flight I saw many people wearing their Boston Marathon jackets from prior years. I hadn't fully realized until then that there were people who had run this race for many years and kept coming back. For me this was going to be a once-in-a-lifetime event.

We arrived in Boston and drove to our hotel in Natick, which is about 20 miles from Boston and very close to the start line.

The next day we went to the Expo to pick up my bib and we spent a lot of time there. It was so powerful to feel all the energy from the people and the runners. I thought the color chosen for the 2014 Boston Marathon jacket was a very strong orange, but I went ahead and bought one anyway, I worked really hard to get there and I wanted to have it as a symbol of the event.

There was a lot of security on the streets, you could see police everywhere. We walked around the finish line and took some photos. We also saw the crosses that had been set up in memory of the people who died in the 2013 Boston Marathon bombing. That was very sad to see.

At the Expo I bought a book called "If Not for the Perfect Stranger" by Tedy Bruschi and Jack Fultz. It was a compilation of many heartwarming stories of kindness from the 2013 Boston Marathon - stories about how people helped each other and risked their own lives to help others.

Memorial of people that lost their lives in the Boston Marathon 2013.

We had the opportunity to go into the Marathon Sports stories near were the first bomb had exploded. Inside the store they had a memorial with flowers and some banners with information that described some of the events that happened near the store.

There were also some cool photos and other items of past famous runners from previous races in that store. They had framed the shirt Steve Prefontaine wore in a race and we saw some of his shoes too.

I had learned about Steve Prefontaine, one of the most famous American runners of all time, who died in a car accident in 1975 at the young age of 24. The world never got to see his highest potential and yet he broke American records and was very accomplished during his far too short life. I had visited his memorial located where his car accident happened in Eugene Oregon.

At the Expo I received a bracelet created from the 2013 Boston Marathon street banners. It was very meaningful to wear it in honor of the people affected by the Boston Marathon bombings.

It was one more day to race and we decided to go to Hopkinton where the starting line was located and took photos at the start and under my corral number. They had what they called the "Runners' Village" from which all runners were required to start on race day.

It was almost .8 mile away from the start line. I thought that was almost an extra mile to add to the marathon.

Boston Marathon starts at Hopkinton every year.

We walked around to find it and to see the relative distance to the start line. After that, we drove the course. I wanted to see how the road was going to be and to have an idea of what the course looked like. We began near the start line. There was a tree there made from shoes in memory of a woman runner who had been killed in an accident. We stopped for a while to look at the memorial.

We continued to drive through the course. We drove to where Jeremy would be around the 10th mile mark. We agreed I was going to run on the left side to try to make contact and to make sure he saw me.

I started to have a pretty good feeling for the course. As we were approaching Newton, which is the city next to Boston, there was a big sign that said: "Training got you to Newton." I thought that was very cute. After we finished driving the marathon route we went for a special dinner at the Boston City Hall. It was quite an experience as it was very cold and we had to wait in a long line to get in. We participated in the dinner and then we headed to the hotel. It was now only a matter of hours...

Boston Race Day

F inally race day had arrived! My first thought of the morning was I am about to run through eight cities, Hopkinton, Ashland, Framingham, Natick, Wellesley, Newton, Brookline, and finish in Boston, and an immediate - YES I am ready! - followed the thought.

Boston Marathon run through eight cities official course map -via baa.org

I got up early as I had signed up for a hotel shuttle that would take me right to the start line. The shuttle left with plenty of time, but we were told we needed to stop at a different site from the original drop off site because that one was already full, so I wondered what that meant.

We got out at that second site and a lot of other runners had been dropped off there as well. The line started to get longer as more and more runners were getting dropped off at that site. Soon a coordinator of the race came over and told us we would be picked up by special buses that would take us to a third site where we were going to be screened for security reasons, and then we would be dropped near the Runner's Village. At that point we would be screened for security again before entering the village.

When we went through the security checks, I felt like I was at the airport, but I'd much rather have this than be in another bombing. Finally, I got to the Runner's Village. I had about half an hour to go before my corral started. I got a water and went to stand in line for the bathroom -- that was all I had time to do. The bathroom lines were long and while waiting there was an announcement made about a military plane that was going to pass in the sky. They were on their way to Boston to be part of the security team in place for the race. That was amazing to see. As I moved to second person in line they started calling my corral, which was just perfect.

I started to move towards my corral and the .8 mile walk began. I removed my jacket and started to put sun screen lotion on as I was walking to the corral. The energy that I felt was incredible. Everybody was smiling and had a sentiment in their eyes like they were saying: "Nothing will stop our spirit, our country, our city."

At the corral waiting for the signal to start, people were so excited they were screaming. Everybody was ready and could hardly wait any longer. There was a great unstoppable, positive energy. Finally, the race started! I had planned to only go at an 8-minute mile pace, but I couldn't contain myself. I looked at my watch and realized I was running too fast, but I couldn't stop. I knew I needed to slow down but the road was going downhill and the people's energy and my own energy were pulling me.

I started to see in more detail what was around me. There were children outside their houses offering me water bottles and there were big signs that said: "your respiration is my inspiration." That was so amazing! There were lines of kids and people waiting to shake the runners' hands -- my hand. I started to shake their hands and was able to slow down that way.

The runners started to spread out, I saw a guy offering beer to runners, and there was even a father with a baby in his arms. I shook the baby's hand and he smiled at me. I could hear the dad say "Yay, a runner shook your hand!" I smiled at them.

During part of the race I remember thinking that it was not long ago, before 1972, when women were not allowed to run marathons, which was about as long as I had been alive.

I have read about women such as Roberta Gibb, who ran the Boston marathon unregistered in 1966, and Kathrine Switzer, who ran Boston registering with her initials K.V. Switzer in 1967. By using initials only, her gender was unclear and thus her registration went through and she received a bib number. Her number was 261. Back then, since only men could enter the race, when the race director discovered there was a woman in the race he tried to remove her bib, but she was defended by other runners in the race.

I felt so lucky to be running this marathon so many brave women had run unregistered in the past. Many, like Kathrine, had opened doors for us to have this opportunity. I also felt so grateful to run this marathon where so many elite athletes had run through these cities of Massachusetts.

I felt I was making my own history in my own personal life, in my own space, and with my very own steps.

I realized the road started to change and there were ups and downs on the road.

I saw Jeremy near mile 8 at Natick, where he say hi and encouraged me and took photos.

Around the 15th mile I started to feel a bit tired. As I was getting close to Newton there was the big sign that said "Training got you to Newton," and close to the 18th mile loomed the big heart-break hill.

I remember seeing the girls at Wellesley College. They were screaming so loud and they had signs for "free kisses" and "the cute ones have run away." Some of the men in the race were talking about kissing one of these girls.

During the run I began to think about the 2013 Boston Marathon bombing. Two of the homemade pressure cooker bombs were detonated near the finish line on Boylston Street. I thought about how difficult that must have been. I thought about the special people who had run the race that day, such as the people who ran for charities, who were probably finishing at the time when the bombings happened. I thought about the people who had died near the race that day during the marathon: Krystle Marie Campbell, 29 years old; Lu Lingzi, 23 years old; and Martin William Richard, who was just 8 years old. I thought about all the wounded people who lost their legs or were injured in other ways.

It is hard to imagine that so much harm could be done to people who had worked so hard, or to people who just loved to observe the human spirit of running a marathon -- people who were not harming anyone, who had big dreams and great aspirations.

At about three miles from the finish line I was desperately looking for the big CITGO sign. I had heard that Boston Marathon runners are often encouraged to look out for the CITGO sign which is situated on the race route one mile from the finish line. I knew that once I saw the sign it would be just a little more before the race would be over. The sign is located high and is visible from a long distance. I felt tired and I wanted to see the sign and feel the victory of finishing such a special race – a feeling that would be with me forever. But then I also thought of all the preparation and all the hard work, and that the beautiful journey would soon be over. I had mixed emotions about getting to the finish line.

CITGO sign located few miles before the finish line, commonly used by runners to know how close they are to the finish line.

Suddenly I saw the sign and then there was an amazing tunnel under a bridge with lights running through it. I tried to run faster as I was passing the tunnel. It was like there was something in the lights that got into me, some sort of energy, and there I was turning right onto Hereford Street. Finally, I

We were there to support each other and to show that we

turned left on Boylston Street and became very emotional as the finish line came into view and I approached it.

I was hoping to finish the race at 3:45, but I realized the course was harder than expected and my time on the day was 3:55. But I had finished the best race of my life up to that point! I was so happy to have finished and I enjoyed every moment of the race. I was part of a movement, the Boston Strong Spirit! Which demonstrated to those who had hurt our runners, our runners' families, our country, and the city of Boston, that our hearts were brave, and our spirits were high. We were there to support each other and to show that we will always continue to run.

At the Boston finished line.

After I finished I got my medal and a very nice, warm blanket. I went to look for Jeremy at the place we had agreed to meet. He had brought some warmer clothes for me to wear. I got warm and asked who won the race. I heard that the men's race had been won by an American for the first time in 39 years and the winner was none other than Meb Keflezighi! He had the names of the three victims of the bombing on his bib. He won the race with an outstanding time of 2:08:37, which was super-fast.

I was really hoping Shalane Flanagan had won the women's race as I had heard so much about her and how hard she had trained but, unfortunately, she did not win. As Meb had said, 'race to win' means doing the best you can do that day. And Shalane did very well, finishing the race with a great time of 2:22:02.

The day after the race we decided to go back to Boston with one objective in mind -- to go to the JFK Library and look for Jeremy's results from when he ran Boston in 1995. We had tried to get the results on the internet previously, but we couldn't find them and we heard going to the library was the only way to get them. At the library we looked for the archive area where they have all the past newspapers, and somebody showed us the microfilms. We were able to look on the machines and we browsed carefully until we found the information. Jeremy had run the 1995 Boston Marathon in 2:47. I felt very proud and I wished I could have been there with him.

When we returned from Boston my family had a celebration for me in Mexico. My sister Lupita made a banner that had my photo, my Boston medal, and a message: "Elba for us you are more than a champion." That message touched my heart.

When I look back at the fact that I went from never having run, to running Boston, one of the oldest and toughest marathons in the world, it makes me feel so blessed. Being able to participate in a marathon run by many elite athletes from around the world, and a marathon so difficult to qualify for, I feel this was more than just a bucket list run. I feel the journey I took, the people who were there with me offering care and words of encouragement, along with the experiences of every training day were all part of achieving this goal. It was not only about running Boston, it was about every step of the process to get there.

I feel this is more than a dream I achieved. It is a story to share with others who also have dreams. Sometimes our dreams may seem crazy or somehow unreachable, so the idea of quitting comes to our minds. But the truth is we can do anything we want to if we have the burning desire, the aspiration inside, and we work hard and believe in ourselves, especially if we surround ourselves with supportive and loving people. There is no shame in falling down and getting up again, even with a broken nose.

2014-2019: Finishing the Running Promise.

2014

After having completed the Boston Marathon, I rested for a few days and then continued my promise to run ten years while fundraising for LLS. I had signed up for the San Diego half marathon race at the beginning of the year.

2014 was my fifth year running for Team In Training and raising funds for cancer research and patient support. My fifth brother, his wife, and my niece were at the race. It was very special to have my brother there watching me run as I celebrated five years of running and helping. My brother has always been an inspiration to me and having him there made the experience even more special.

By this time, my participation in the long runs with Team In Training was not as consistent as for my earlier races due to other commitments in my personal life and at work. However, if I didn't attend the Saturday group run I would do a solo long run on Sunday of the same planned distance.

I knew Meb Keflezighi was going to be in the race and I heard he was going to do a friendly run of three miles the day before the marathon. I decided to sign up as I was hoping to get his signature on my Boston bib.

The experience was outstanding! Running with Meb was amazing! He was going much slower than he would normally, and I was running as fast as I could so I could stay in the front and continue to run with him. A lot of people asked him questions about his career, his times, and many other things. Around the second mile I got the chance to get close and I told him that he was a huge inspiration to me and I was a Team In Training person. He said "thank you" and asked for my name, I told him and he smiled.

As we were approaching the last 200 meters of the run someone asked him if he would sprint from the 100 meter mark to the end. That was it for me though. I saw them run very fast and I kept my pace until I finished. Meb did end up signing my Boston bib that day though - he wrote: "Was nice to share the Boston roads with you, run to win."

Photo by Claudia Armenta.

That same day at the Inspiration Dinner Meb was present to support LLS runners and he gave a wonderful speech where he spoke about his Boston Marathon victory and how hard it was to get to that point in his running journey. He mentioned the time when his father risked all, including his life, to fight for a future for his family. I had invited my best friend, her husband and my family to attend the dinner with me. We were all inspired when he spoke about his own personal struggles in life and about the meaning that comes from helping patients and families living with cancer.

Throughout my running to that point I had thought about how being female runner was special. It came to my mind often that running long distance was a male only sport for a long time. But I was part of a change happening where more women were participating in this great sport. It was the year I was born that things started to change for women. My life began to transform the moment I knew about running and started to do it. This transformation was good in all areas of my life, not only physical or emotional, but even at work.

I knew running was good for me and I couldn't stop thinking about how many women were not yet aware of the benefits of running? How many women still do not believe they can do it? I have especially thought about women in the country I was born. Why didn't I see more women running when I was going growing up? But also how much of a difference running is making for women now?

It was in 2014 when I had the idea to start writing my journey of running and my running promise, to share it with others in hope that maybe other women will learn and grow in running as I had. I had also thought that there will be a time in the future when I can no longer run, and perhaps I could forget the wonderful details of my experiences. I didn't want that to happen. I wanted to remember. I thought that writing would keep my memories close to me and hopefully encourage others especially other women. I also thought I could share my journey with the people that had supported me as a form of gratitude.

Coincidentally it was this year that I also had the good fortune to run the San Diego Rock 'n' Roll race with some wonderful women from work who shared my love of running. It was nice to see that there were more and more women running long distance and I was delighted to be one with them. I was also happy that one of them was a supporter for my fundraising and encouraged my passion for helping people with cancer through Team In Training.

2014 at the Expo picking up race bibs with other women.

During this time I also thought about my mother, growing up in Sinaloa Mexico she never had the opportunity to experience running or any other sports. Not only because it was not part of her culture and time but because her life was difficult. She was born in 1931 and at the age of nine my grandmother become ill with what we believe was cancer too, my mom was forced to leave school to provide care. After losing her mother to this terrible illness her life was about survival until she met my father and formed a family on her own. I remember her being good at mathematics and having a competitive spirit. My imagination could not stop wondering: if the conditions of her life would have been different would she had like running? If things had been different perhaps she would had been able to run and compete. Perhaps she would have loved running as much as I do.

The half way mark of my ten-year promise in 2014 was very special and I will never forget it.

2015

Year six came faster than I thought it would. My new year began with signing up for the 2015 race and starting to plan what I would do for the year. The plan was the same as the previous year. Sign up, start the webpage for fundraising, and start receiving the Team In Training plan for each week of running. I received the meeting time and date for the long runs, but again I would not make every Saturday run and ended up doing many solo runs on Sundays.

Long runs on Sunday.

My Sunday solo runs were moments of reflection and peace for me after very busy weeks at work. During my running time I would use positive thinking to energize my mind at the same time I was exercising my body.

When I was able to make it to run with the team I would feel grateful to enjoy a long run with others and to hear the stories that fueled the inspiration behind my passion to continue running.

I was connected with the team through Facebook and was able to keep in touch with the team members during the week as well.

During long training runs Jeremy sometimes would ride his bike and bring water, a very nice gesture that would always make me smile. Sometime we would run together.

Every year I ran with an IN HONOR OF or IN MEMORY OF sign on my shirt. My mom's name was Magdalena and sometimes I wrote, "I run for Magdalena," or, "I run for my mom," or I would just write her name.

Fundraising became harder and harder. I used Facebook as a source of connecting with friends and family who were able to help me reach my goal. I would start fund raising at the beginning of January and continue until May. If I didn't have enough, I would make up the difference myself. I would share some special moments on Facebook with the people who helped me, such as a special thank you note or the distance I had run.

One of the great things about running the Rock 'n' Roll series every year is that each race has live music throughout the route. Every two or three miles there would be a band. This was so encouraging and on many occasions helped me keep the pace. Unique to San Diego, a certain section of the route has drummers perform, which is very special. The drum sounds can be felt in the heart and it is hard to describe in words, but the sound creates a reaction, even stronger than the music itself, and pushes you to move forward, to move at a harder pace, and to feel more energized. I was thankful for those musicians who volunteered to help create this feeling in runners like me.

Drummers at the San Diego Rock 'n' Roll race route. Photo by Claudia Armenta.

During the 2015 San Diego Rock 'n' Roll event I met a great woman. She was 92 years old and her name is Harriette Thompson. She was part of the Team In Training group raising money for cancer and she had done so for 16 years. She was survivor. This was a very special race for her because she had broken the record as the oldest woman who had completed a full marathon. She did it in a little over 7 hours. She never saw herself as an unusual or unique, but she was an inspiration for me and so many other people.

She showed us all that there is no age at which you should stop dreaming or trying to better yourself, that we should all pursue our dreams, and should work hard to achieve them regardless of any preconceived notions.

Other years I had run, with the exception of 2013 I had received a race medal. But this year, similarly to 2013 I received two medals! The normal medal for the year, and the most special of all the medals I have received and I believe I will ever receive -- the "Run for Charity" medal. It was special in the sense that it represented the reason for running. It was not about speed or time or distance but it represented the achievement of the goal to HELP, and to make a difference.

At the beginning of this book I shared how I started to run later in life, and up until now my experience had been long distance running. I began to wonder what shorter distance track and field would feel like. I had never tried running on a track before and I was curious to try the track at least once. I heard there was going to be an "ALL COMERS" track meet in San Diego and decided to sign up for one race. I chose to run the 5K, at a meet held at San Diego State University. I had run 5K on the road many times but never on a track. It was a very unique experience. The race was at night with rainy conditions. It was not really raining, but more misty humid weather. Any person can compete in these track meets: any age, any level. This was a very enjoyable experience. Some of races were very fun to watch, like the one where kids of different ages competed.

2016

I attended the Olympic Trials in 2016 at the University of Oregon in Eugene. It was an amazing experience to be able to see such exceptional runners compete in these races! It can be difficult for these athletes when all the effort of many days and years of training comes down to a single moment when it is decided who will represent our country in the Olympics. I learned that the person who advances is not necessarily better than the others, but that they were better in that moment at that race. There are many other factors that contribute as well. I enjoyed watching the short distance track and field races. I saw Alyson Felix, Brenda Martinez, and many other great elite runners compete, win, and, in some cases, lose. It was very inspiring. Experiencing the Olympic Trials was particularly meaningful for me because I had tried running on the track the year before. I learned that losing may sometimes bring out the best of who you are as a person. If you recall what happened in the women's 800 meters finals at the 2016 Olympic Trials, you will know what I mean - especially with regards to Brenda Martinez and Alysia Montano. They were both favorites to win the race, but Brenda Martinez tripped, collided with Alysia Montano, and took a hard fall with less than 150m to go. The winner of the race was Olympic Trials Champion

Kate Grace, but both Brenda and Alysia were grateful in defeat.

The beginning of 2016 was a time where I was not sure if I should continue with my ten year goal of running and fundraising for LLS. It felt like I had been at it for a long time and I thought that maybe I should find a different way of helping others.

Many years ago, my mom gave me a tiny teddy bear and I chose to keep it close to me for a little while as I considered whether or not I should stop.

While still trying to make this decision, I was in a Toastmaster club meeting and met a young woman who spoke about her own experience and how she was diagnosed with leukemia when she was nine years old. She told the group what LLS had done for her and her family, and how it was something she will never forget. After her presentation had ended I shared with her I had been part of Team In Training in previous years. She told me she appreciated what I had done to help others. It was in that moment I decided to continue with my original goal of ten years and signed up for another season.

Something special happened during the 2016 San Diego Rock 'n' Rock half marathon around the 8th mile. A girl who was running saw my Team In Training shirt and asked me if I was running for LLS. I told her I was and started to run next to her. She then mentioned her father had died earlier in the year, and with tears in her eyes, told me she was running in his memory. She also thanked me for my contributions to LLS. She said it was very difficult to experience a serious illness like her father had, but it was nice to know there were people who cared and did what they could to help. When she said that, it felt it was the reaffirmation I needed to continue with my promise for the years to come.

I was very impressed with the statistics published about the Rock 'n' Roll San Diego Marathon in 2016. Fifty-seven percent of the people registered in the race were female, and that was a very special moment for women and women runners in our city.

2017

At the start of 2017, I wanted to do something different and decided to set a different goal for the year. I decided to run four races: the San Diego Rock 'n' Roll Marathon to support LLS, and then three more races. The goal for those three races was different: it was to run with my friend Jeremy. We decided to choose from the Rock 'n' Roll series and picked Nashville, Las Vegas, and San Antonio - in that order.

The Nashville race was in April 29th, and during this time my family was notified that my nephew Sammy had collapsed in a store. He was alert after his collapse, but when the paramedics rushed him to the hospital he started to have seizures and ultimately strokes. After the traumatic experience of being in a coma and almost losing his life, he spent a long time in the CCU at the hospital fighting for his recovery. A Coronary Care Unit (CCU) is a hospital place that specializes in the care of patients with heart attacks, and various other cardiac disorders that require continuous monitoring and treatment.

The race was so close to the day this happened that we almost did not run, but we decided to run in his honor. Thus, while he was still in the hospital in a coma, Jeremy and I left for the weekend just to do the race and return. My niece Sandra, Sammy's sister, joined us in Nashville, so we could run together, even though she had also just been at the hospital in California. Sandra and I agreed to make a prayer for his recovery after each mile that we ran, and the three of us, Jeremy, Sandra and I had a sticker in our shirt that said: "I run for Sammy". Miraculously, he survived and is well today.

I ran the Rock 'n' Roll San Diego half marathon on June 4th. You may remember I mentioned that during my 2015 San Diego Rock 'n' Roll race I met Harriette Thompson who was 92 at that time. In 2017 she ran again but this time a half marathon and at the age of 94 she become the oldest woman to run a half marathon. She was a true inspiration for me. We had the same goal to raise funds to find the cure for cancer and she did an awesome job with her own fundraising to support Leukemia and Lymphoma Society.

During the Expo I saw Meb Keflezighi and he signed my Bib with a message that said: "To Elba, Best Wishes, God Is Good, Run to Win. Meb". Before he signed it I had asked him if he could add the "God Is Good".

The Las Vegas race was a special one as well as it is a race that happens at night in the month of November. Again, one of the things the Rock 'n' Roll series is popular for is having live music along the course. And there were many bands playing at different mile markers. A few weeks before we went, there was a horrific mass shooting in Las Vegas at a music festival. Fifty eight people were kill and 422 were wounded. Because of this there was a mile of silence near the place where the shooting had taken place which was very meaningful. The strip with all the full color and light was completely silence except for the sound of the runner's steps. During the Vegas race on November 12th, I selected a small sign to run with that said: "IN HONOR OF: October 1st

Victims". Many people had similar messages that said: "Vegas Strong". " At the Expo I saw Meb Keflezighi again and he signed my Bib for the second time that year.

The San Antonio race was at the end of the year in December. It was a very special race for me too as it culminated my goal for the year. There was a mariachi band in the race along with other bands, and while we were running the first four miles, it started to rain. Running in the rain was fun. It was not as cold as I thought it might be and this race ended up being a great experience.

During the Expo I had the opportunity to meet Kathrine Switzer - the first woman to run the Boston Marathon as a registered runner – in person, and it was a wonderful privilege! I learned she had started a running club called 261, which was her bib number when she ran that first race in 1967. She had run the Boston Marathon again in 4/16/2017 at the age of 70, 50 years later.

I was enthralled by the river walk in San Antonio, especially because it was Christmas time, and there were lights creating a shimmery effect in the water. It was a wonderful way to mark the end of 2017.

2018

This race marked my ninth year running with Team In Training. It was extra special to me as it would be only one more year before the journey would come to an end, and somehow it made me feel emotional already. I trained from January to June as I would normally. It was nice to get to know people who were just starting to run.

After 9 years, many changes had happened. I had run with different groups of couches and met many runners. People that were special to me had retired at LLS and the race was no longer the large LLS event that it has been at least not in San Diego. There were other larger US events in other cities, but San Diego was no longer included. Despite all of this, there was an option to run for LLS in San Diego and there was a small team that would meet and train. The support of the team was there and I could still support people with cancer like other years, thus I signed up one more year.

It was good to see the support of my friends along the way as well.

It had been nine years running with Team In Training and 2019 would mark the "ten year running promise" - a goal to run the San Diego Rock 'n' Roll marathon or half marathon for cancer fundraising 10 consecutive years; a goal that I had set for myself to help others. To add to my goal, I decided to continue writing about my journey, with the objective of publishing the story sometime in 2019 or 2020.

In 2018 I ran the Vegas Rock 'n' Roll for the second time. I enjoyed running at night, something that was different from my other races. It was nice to see the Vegas lights while running. During the race, however; I experienced stomach problems for the first time while running and had one of my slowest races. It was the first time that I had to stop for a few minutes during a race. After the race was over I was not sure if I wanted to run at night again. But after some time and after feeling better I decided to try again the following year, and planned to be more careful with my food intake.

2019

S ince the beginning of the year, 2019 had been a year of reflection. I knew it would be my year to fulfill a promise: The Running Promise.

I realize ten years seemed like a long time when I started, but I now feel it was never about the ten years, it was about the journey that has helped me grow: the journey that took me to different places to meet so many people and that helped me to enrich my life in a way I would have never thought possible.

So far, through the years since the beginning of this journey I have raised more than $14,000 dollars to support LLS, I have run more than 4000 miles, and I have learned and experienced many stories that have touched my heart.

This is my own personal story where the power of perseverance, consistency, and hope moved me from within the deepest part of myself, and I hope this story might inspire others to chase their dreams.

If you are afraid, remember everyone else is too, but act despite the fear because behind that fear there is an unleashed power ready to help when you need it most. A power that will come to you when you decide to act. A power that will transform you, a power that will take you there. When you decide to pursue your dreams, you will find there are people there to help you. Setting your goals is just the beginning of the journey, but what is to come will be marvelous, extraordinary and life fulfilling. What is to come is finding your happiness.

I hope to continue to run in the future, not necessarily the Rock 'n' Roll marathon series, but to continue to help others even if not through LLS, but perhaps through other means.

I encourage you to think about what deliberate practice can bring to you and how to achieve your goals. I recommend reading the book *Talent is Overrated* by Geoff Colvin, to improve performance in any field or in any area of your life. A few thoughts have stuck with me from this book: We need to think about four main things. First we need to have a plan to practice. A plan that can be adjusted as you learn and focus on the areas you need to improve on.

The second is having a coach or mentor. Someone who knows how things work and has the experience to help you. Someone you trust that will have your best interests in mind but at the same time will help you push your limits, and most importantly, someone who helps you identify those areas of focus for your plan, so you can drive success.

The third is accepting feedback. We all have blind spots we cannot see, and we need others to help us see. As we listen and take feedback, we adjust our plan and we do things differently until we get the results we are going after. However, it takes acceptance to listen to someone telling us we are doing it wrong and to have the will power to accept our mistakes and change what we do to really become better.

The fourth is repetition. Execute the plan and the activity that will make you better over and over without giving up. It will get better as you continue to practice. We need to recognize it is not always fun, and sometimes there will be pain and sweat, and setbacks. But if we know this and we are willing to keep our goals, then we can go far in accomplishing them.

In the moments of repetition of what you want to improve on, when there is pain, and doubt; when you have to get up early when everyone else is sleeping, when you have to spend a whole Sunday doing a long run and recovering, when you get injured and have to go back to the gym to maintain your cardio level, when all those things tell you it is easier to quit, it is good to remember what Geoff Colvin mentioned in his book.

As I prepared for what I thought might be my last run on the streets of San Diego fundraising for cancer research, I also kept thinking of what would be next. I did not have an answer for that yet, but perhaps I will run more, donate my time, or find an alternate way to raise funds.

Last words to my Mom

My message to my Mom as I prepared to finish the Rock 'n' Roll San Diego race in 2019:

"Mom, some people believe you are not here, I believe you have always been. I believe you live in me and you help me to achieve goals I once thought were impossible for me to achieve. You have always been here and you help me be a better human being, stronger every day, happier every day. Get ready Mom, we will finish this race in 2019 for the last time. I promise, I love you."

Last Words to You

Believe you can, pursue your dreams, transform yourself to who you want to be, and run hard towards your own finish line. And when you cross it, share your story.

Ten Years! - 2010

Ten Years! - 2011

Ten Years! - 2012

Ten Years! - 2013

Ten Years! - 2014

Ten Years! - 2015

Ten Years! - 2016

Ten Years! - 2017

Ten Years! - 2018

Ten Years! - 2019

Over 30,000 People run the San Diego Rock 'n' Roll 2019 race. I was one of them. To me it was special. I finished my 10 year running promised.
My Team was able to race 37,000 dollars to support cancer this year.

Thank you Roberto, Ana Maria, Lulu, Pennie, Sandra, Anabel, Bella, Miguel Angel, Claudia, Jeremy, Patty, Nery, Teo, Emiliano and Julio for been there.

Recommended Resources:

Books

Run to Overcome, Meb Keflezighi.
If Not for the Perfect Stranger, Tedy Bruschi and Jack Fultz.
How to Train For and Run Your Best Marathon, Gordon Bakoulis.
Marathon Woman, Kathrine Switzer.
Life is an Ultramarathon, Dixie Madsen.
Talent is Overrated, Geoff Colvin.
The One Thing, Gary W. Keller and Jay Papasan.
Go Giver, Bob Burg and John David Mann.
Awaken the Giant Within, Anthony Robins.
Unlimited Power, Anthony Robins.
Inner Simplicity, Elaine St. James.
Essentialism, Greg McKeon.
Outliers, Malcom Gladwell.
Brain Rules, John Medina.
Strength Finder, Tom Rath.
Getting Things Done, David Allen.
25 Ways to win with people, John Maxwell.
The Charisma Edge, Cynthia Burnham.

Apps:

Think up
Garmin Connect
MyFitnessPal

Podcast:
The One Thing
My Thought Coach

Index:

About the author:

Elba Watkins is a Manager in an Engineering Company. She earned her Engineering Degree from the Autonomous University of Baja California, Mexico in 1995 and holds several certifications from the American Society of Quality (ASQ). She has worked in manufacturing environments for over 20 years. During her school years Elba took clarinet classes and other art classes but never was part of any sport. She began running long races in 2010 to support people with cancer through the Leukemia and Lymphoma Society (LLS). So far she had run several Rock 'n' Roll races including San Diego California, Los Angeles California, Phoenix Arizona, Nashville Tennessee, Las Vegas Nevada, and San Antonio Texas. In 2014 she qualified for and ran the Boston Marathon. She believes running transformed her personal and professional life. She sees running as the catalyst for mental change to be positive and to be happy.

The Running Promise

Made in USA - Kendallville, IN
1085381_9781696790352
04.22.2020 0909